Christmas at Home

101 Family Activities for the Holidays

written and compiled by
Ellyn Sanna

BARBOUR
PUBLISHING, INC.
Uhrichsville, Ohio

Making Christmas Memories

Christmas is a special time, a time of excitement, wonder, and love. As adults, however, too often we allow our Christmas joy to be dimmed by the weight of holiday chores and long shopping lists; we let the hassle of holiday crowds cloud our hearts with impatience; and we forget about the quiet wonder of a newborn Baby.

This book has some suggestions for ways you and your family can recapture your sense of Christmas joy. Don't try to do all 101 activities (or you'll end up more hassled and stressed than ever), but pick and choose those that specially speak to you. Most of all, these activities are designed to include the whole family. Christmas is a time to share our love, making special memories to last a lifetime.

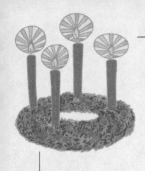

Behold, a virgin shall be with child,
and shall bring forth a son,
and they shall call his name Emmanuel,
which being interpreted is,
God with us.

MATTHEW 1:23

Nativity Scenes

Put a nativity scene under your Christmas tree—or on the mantel or the top of a bookshelf. Try to find one that is not too fragile or valuable. Spend time with your children talking about it. Encourage them to interact with it using their imaginations.

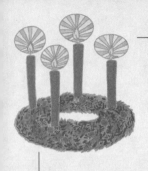

Christmas
Picture Book

Make a Christmas card book for your young children—or have your older children make books that can be shared with a preschool class or young Sunday school class. Erase or remove the signatures on four old Christmas cards and open them out flat. Stack the cards on top of each other in the same

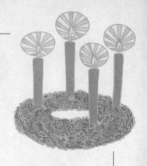

direction so that all the pictures are facing down on the same side. Sew the cards together along the crease and refold to form the book. Press the cards with a heavy book if necessary to make them lie flat.

MATERIALS:
old Christmas cards   needle and thread

Handprint Cards

A unique way to share your family's Christmas wishes with friends is with a special handmade card. First, have the father use a colored pencil to trace around his hand on a sheet of paper. Next, have the mother trace her hand inside the outline of her husband's. Then trace around the children's hands, each inside the outlines of the others. Use different colors for each

person. Add Christmas greetings to complete your distinctively personalized card.

MATERIALS:
paper
colored markers

Angels, from the realms of glory,
Wing your flight o'er all the earth;
Ye who sang creation's story,
Now proclaim Messiah's birth:
Come and worship, come and worship,
Worship Christ, the newborn King.

JAMES MONTGOMERY, 1816

A Christmas Remembrance

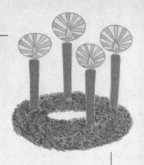

For those Christmases touched by the loss of a loved one, don't let sadness take away all the joy of the season. Decorate a houseplant with a bow or evergreen and set the plant near a family photo. In the midst of your sorrow, remember the joys shared with that person, the happiness of past Christmases. Christmas is a point of connection between our present here on earth and our future in eternity.

Advent Wreath

Make an Advent wreath with your family. Fasten four candle-holders into an evergreen wreath. Drill holes into a board or set holders into a plaster of paris mold to make sure they are secure. Cover the base with damp sand to keep the evergreen branches alive longer. The traditional colors for the candles are three purple and one rose (to be used on the third Sunday). Some people, however, like to use all red candles, or all white or all purple. Light

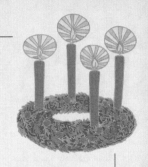

one candle on the first Sunday in Advent and another each Sunday until all the candles are lit. Make this a special time of prayer and song.

MATERIALS:
4 candles   evergreen branches
board or plaster of paris   sand

Love Box

Create a Love Box and keep it throughout the year. All year, collect items in the box that could be used as gifts at Christmastime. Encourage your children to make their own additions to the box (for example, their "Happy Meal" toys). When Christmas comes, the items in this box can provide gifts for families in your community, even those you don't know as well. Another possible use for the Love Box is to collect in it things to give to a specific ministry or mission.

*A*nd she brought forth her firstborn son,
and wrapped him in swaddling clothes,
and laid him in a manger;
because there was no room for them in the inn.

LUKE 2:7

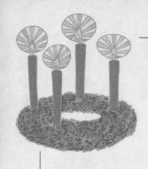

Forced Flowers

Bring branches of flowering trees into your home to make them bloom. Bring the branches in on December 4 and stand them in water in a warm room. As it gets closer to Christmas, the flowers will bloom, a symbol of Christ who gives life to us. Talk to your children about the special meaning of this Christmas tradition.

Spiritual Housecleaning

Clean out your heart to make room for Christ. Christmas is a good time to get rid of all the anger, bitterness, and negative emotions that you have been carrying around. Without such things you can better enjoy the happiness of Christmas and can truly sing that there is room in your heart for Jesus. As a family, make a point of talking about the things for which you are sorry, asking each other's forgiveness.

Wheat Plants

Grow wheat for the Christ Child. This is an old Hungarian tradition. Wheat seeds are planted in small pots on December 13. The pots are kept in a warm room and the seeds watered daily. On Christmas Eve, the growing plants are brought to the

nativity scene and placed beside the manger. The plants symbolize that the Christ who is coming is the Bread of Life.

MATERIALS:
wheat seeds   small pots
planting soil

Hark, *the herald angels sing,*
  "Glory to the newborn King;
Peace on earth, and mercy mild,
  God and sinners reconciled!"
Joyful, all ye nations rise,
  Join the triumph of the skies;
With th' angelic host proclaim,
  "Christ is born in Bethlehem."

SAMUEL WESLEY, 1739

Christmas Cookies

Do Christmas baking together. There are a large variety of traditional Christmas cookies and sweetbreads from around the world, many of which have symbolic meanings. An example is *lebkuchen*, the German "life cakes," which symbolize new life in Christ. Doing the baking as a family lets children feel included and adds to the family closeness.

Intangible Gifts

Teach your children that gifts don't have to be material things. Have them make ornaments from construction paper, cutting the paper in the shape of a stocking or an old-fashioned shoe. Cut out two of each form and have the child glue all the edges together except the top. Fasten a ribbon to the top corner in order to hang the ornament from the tree. The real gift, however, is a folded piece of paper inside the ornament on

which the child writes a promise of something she will do for someone—for her brother or sister, her mother or father. In this way she learns that gifts of time are also legitimate gifts.

MATERIALS:
colored construction paper ribbon
glue paper and pen

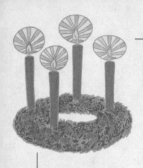

Baby Gifts

Give to a local pregnancy center. Jesus was born poor and homeless, seemingly illegitimate. Why not bring baby gifts to a pregnancy center for other children who are possibly poor, homeless, or illegitimate as well? Your children might want to pick out some of their old baby toys or books to give, and they will enjoy shopping with you for other items. As a family, pray for the children who will receive the gifts.

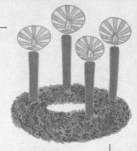

*G*lory to God in the highest,
and on earth peace, good will toward men.

LUKE 2:14

Christ Tree

Make a Christian Christmas tree. On such a tree, all the decorations relate to the Bible or church history. Ornaments could include: angels, doves, a twelve-pointed star, a lamb, candles, a rainbow, grapes, an ark, scrolls, and whatever other ideas your family comes up with. Martin Luther was the first to celebrate the Nativity with a "Christ tree."

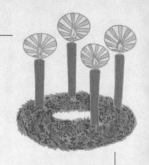

Christmas Drives

Take a drive to see the Christmas lights. Bundle the kids into warm pajamas and blankets and tuck them into the car. Go out late at night so few other cars will be on the road and drive around slowly to see as many lights and decorations as you can. You might want to sing carols as you go.

"The Nutcracker"

Take your children to see "The Nutcracker Suite." They will be delighted by this Christmas ballet.

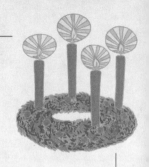

It came upon the midnight clear,
That glorious song of old,
From angels bending near the earth,
To touch their harps of gold:
"Peace on the earth, good will to men,
From heaven's all-gracious King."
The world in solemn stillness lay
To hear the angels sing.

EDMOND HAMILTON SEARS, 1834

Piñata

This is a Mexican tradition, which is part of the Christmas celebration. The piñata is filled with candy and small presents and hung from the ceiling. Children are blindfolded, spun around, and given three tries to break open the piñata with a broom handle.

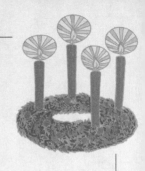

MATERIALS:
round balloon, inflated
flowerpot
water
acrylic paint
white glue

petroleum jelly
1 cup flour
newspaper
colored tissue paper
ribbons, 2 inches wide

Piñata Directions:

Rub a thin coating of petroleum jelly over the balloon and balance balloon, tied end down, in the flowerpot. Mix water slowly with the flour until paste is the consistency of pancake batter. Tear newspaper into 2-inch strips and immerse strips in paste. Cover the balloon with the newspaper strips until all but the end in the flowerpot is covered.

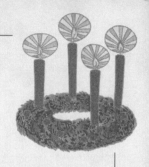

Add two more layers of newspaper and let dry completely (about 24 hours). Pop the balloon and wipe out any excess petroleum jelly, then dry another 24 hours. Paint the piñata with acrylic paint and glue ribbons and tissue paper streamers to the bottom. Use an awl to punch three holes in the rim of the piñata and run strings through the holes for hanging.

Christmas Photos

Start an annual Christmas album. Take a picture of the whole family, including pets. Put the picture in an album and each year add a similar picture. This way the family can appreciate their growth from year to year.

*The shepherds said one to another,
Let us now go even unto Bethlehem,
and see this thing which is come to pass,
which the Lord hath made known unto us.
And they came with haste, and found Mary,
and Joseph, and the babe lying in a manger.*

LUKE 2:15–16

Story Time

Collect Christmas storybooks. Get as many different kinds as you can—books about the Christmas story, *Frosty the Snowman*, *The Christmas Carol*. During the Christmas season, read them to your children at bedtime.

Christmas Hospitality

Have a progressive dinner for families. This saves you and your friends from each having to host a separate meal. Start at one house for appetizers, move on to another for soup and salad, then to another for the main course, and end at the last house for coffee and dessert.

Time Capsule

At your family gathering, put together a time capsule to be opened in five years or more. In a waterproof container, put the front page of that day's newspaper and a list of everyone present (or a Polaroid of everyone). Get everyone to write down a wish and a prediction to add to the capsule. Add whatever other items you think of, such as children's drawings, jewelry, or an audio tape. Bury it in the attic or the garage to be opened on the Christmas of the year you've chosen.

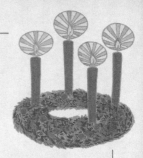

Something New

Make it your family tradition that each year you do something brand new, something your family has never done before, to celebrate the new life Christ brings. This could be skiing, ice skating, visiting a nursing home, going caroling as a family, putting on a Christmas skit—anything that is new for your family. Some experiences you may not want to repeat—and some you may find you want to add to the Christmas traditions you celebrate every year.

*J*oy to the world! The Lord is come;
Let earth receive her King;
Let every heart prepare Him room,
And heaven and nature sing.

ISAAC WATTS, 1719

Sharing the Joy

Help out an elderly neighbor. Help him decorate his home, and fill his refrigerator for him. Drive him to Christmas services if he desires.

Hospital Cheer

Bring decorated baskets of Christmas treats to hospital patients, especially those who won't be able to spend Christmas with their families. Make sure your children help you pack and decorate the baskets.

MATERIALS:
small wicker baskets
  (can usually be bought cheaply from a craft store)
Christmas ribbons   fresh fruits
candy   magazines
scented lotion   paperback books

Christmas Volunteers

Volunteer at a soup kitchen. God has blessed you, perhaps you could spend Christmas Eve ministering to those less fortunate than yourself. Don't forget to bring the whole family along.

In the beginning was the Word,
and the Word was with God,
and the Word was God.
The same was in the beginning with God.
All things were made by him;
and without him was not any thing made that was made.
In him was life; and the life was the light of men.
And the light shineth in darkness;
and the darkness comprehended it not.

JOHN 1:1–5

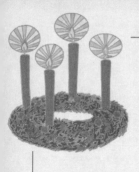

Christmas Charity

Your extended family might want to decide to give to charities instead of giving gifts. In the names of family members, donate to whatever various charities you have chosen ahead of time. Or you might want to take on a special family in need, using the money you would have ordinarily spent on each other to cheer another family's Christmas.

Plenty for Everyone

Invite a family staying at a local shelter to share Christmas dinner with your family.

Christmas Parties

Organize a Christmas party at a nursing home. The residents will enjoy the celebration.

Use Your
Organizational Skills

Help start a canned food drive at your church or a toy drive with your local police or fire department. Another idea is a coat and blanket drive to help homeless or needy people.

O little town of Bethlehem,
How still we see thee lie;
Above thy deep and dreamless sleep
The silent stars go by.
Yet in thy dark streets shineth
The everlasting Light;
The hopes and fears of all the years
Are met in thee tonight.

PHILLIPS BROOKS, 1868

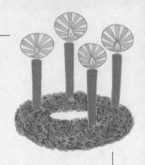

Be a Baby-Sitter

Donate your baby-sitting services to someone who can't afford to pay a baby-sitter. Let a busy mom do some Christmas shopping or have some special time alone with her husband. Her kids and yours can have a special evening or weekend together, eating popcorn and watching Christmas videos.

Christmas Newsletter

Send a family newsletter along with your Christmas cards. Write about your family's activities and achievements from throughout the past year. Older children can write their own stories; younger ones can dictate to you what they want to share. Add black and white photographs, artwork, and designs. If you don't have a computer capable of handling the graphics, go to a copy shop to have copies made.

Take a Break

Don't let the rush and hurry of shopping and activities get to you. Take some time out as a family to do something relaxing. Spend some time reading to the children or play a game together. Make sure that this time to quietly relax together is part of each year's Christmas traditions.

Out and About

Take your family to see or participate in the various ways your community is celebrating the real meaning of Christmas. This could involve visiting nativity scenes or attending church pageants or joining an organized caroling outing to a retirement village.

And the Word was made flesh,
and dwelt among us,
(and we beheld his glory,
the glory as of the only begotten of the Father,)
full of grace and truth.

JOHN 1:14

God's Word

Display the Bible in a special place during the Christmas season. Leave it open to one of the passages that tell of the first Christmas. Make sure the Bible remains a focal point throughout your celebrations.

Christmas Bazaars

Organize and contribute to a Christmas bazaar at church. You can sell handmade ornaments or candy or cookies. The children can help in preparing the items for the sale. Profits can be used to send a special Christmas gift to missionaries overseas.

Decorate!

Decorate your home for Christmas. Sometimes the tree is the only decorating that gets done, along with perhaps a couple of candles on the dining room table. Try to make as much of your home look Christmasy as you can. You don't have to spend a lot of money on decorations; look around and see what you already have to use. Get the children involved with making ornaments (paper chains, cranberries and popcorn on a string, etc.) and hanging them around the house.

Recycled Gifts

Find new things tucked away in your house that you can give as gifts. We often buy things on impulse and then realize later that they are the wrong color or style or size. Sometimes we return them, but at other times we just stick them in a drawer and forget about them. Look around for such things to give; after all, they aren't doing you any good. Get your children involved, sorting through their toys for perfectly good items that are seldom used.

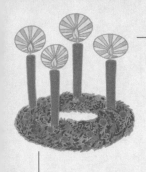

S̲ilent night! Holy night!
All is calm, all is bright,
Round yon virgin mother and Child.
Holy Infant, so tender and mild,
Sleep in heavenly peace,
Sleep in heavenly peace.

JOSEPH MOHR, 1818

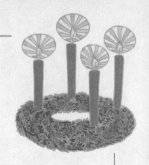

The Gift of Gratitude

Write thank-you letters. During Christmas, make sure you write down what everyone received from whom. After Christmas, get the family together and write notes to thank those friends and relatives who have given to you. In this way you teach your children the importance of a simple thank you.

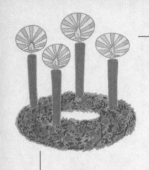

Christmas
with a Theme

Center your Christmas celebrations around a theme. You could choose a country, for example, and learn all you can about that country. Make foods that come from the country you choose and try out some of their Christmas traditions. Experiment with different types of themes—antique toys, musical instruments, etc.

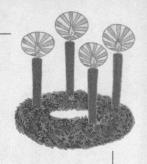

A Gift a Day

Make an Advent calendar. Start with December 1 and continue through Christmas Eve or Christmas Day. Place a little gift for each member of the family in a bag under each date. Or you might want to write a special message or a Bible verse. Use your own ideas to make your Advent calendar unique.

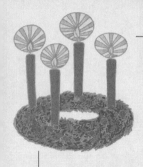

O Tannebaum!

Make the decorating of the tree an event. Get the whole family involved. Play Christmas music and finish off with a Christmasy meal or dessert.

*W*here is he that is born King of the Jews?
*for we have seen his star in the east,
and are come to worship him.*

MATTHEW 2:2

The Messiah

Listen to *The Messiah*. Even better, go to a performance of it. Before hand, explain to your children what they will be hearing and what each section means.

Secret Angels

A week or two before Christmas, draw names among your family. For the remaining time before Christmas, give occasional small gifts to that person and try to be especially kind and helpful to him or her. Nobody can tell whose name they drew until you all reveal them together on Christmas Eve.

Homemade Wrapping Paper

Instead of buying wrapping paper, use brown paper bags to make your own. You and your children can decorate the paper with paint, markers, or rubber stamps. Another idea is to wrap gifts in sheets of comics from the newspaper.

MATERIALS:
brown paper bags
markers, crayons,
  or tempera paint

scissors
stamps and stamp pads

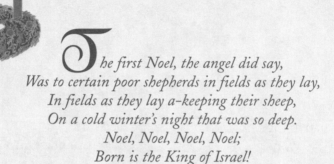

The first Noel, the angel did say,
Was to certain poor shepherds in fields as they lay,
In fields as they lay a-keeping their sheep,
On a cold winter's night that was so deep.
Noel, Noel, Noel, Noel;
Born is the King of Israel!

ANONYMOUS, 17TH CENTURY

A Time of Song

Invite another family or two over and sing Christmas carols together. Remember, Christmas activities don't have to be complicated or time-consuming. Sometimes the best times are the simplest.

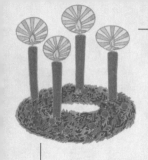

Yule Log

Get a log that has been split down the center, then smooth off the flat edge so that it will sit on a table without wobbling. Using a drill, make two or three holes in the rounded side, big enough to use as candle holders. Decorate the log with ribbons and pinecones and use it as a centerpiece. If you have a fireplace, on Christmas Day you might want to burn your log. Traditionally, each family member writes down the things he or she is sorry for doing over the past year. These are shared among the family, and then one by one the pieces of paper are burned in the Yule fire, symbolizing the total forgiveness we have in Christ.

MATERIALS:

12- to 18-inch log, split in half	drill
pinecones	ribbons
	candles

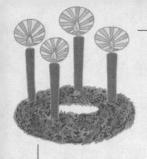

Candlelight

Have a candlelight dinner for Christmas Eve. Try to have as few electric lights as possible, making the most of the candles. Talk with your children about Christ, who is the Light of the world.

or unto us a child is born, unto us a son is given:
and the government shall be upon his shoulder:
and his name shall be called Wonderful, Counsellor,
The mighty God, The everlasting Father,
The Prince of Peace.

ISAIAH 9:6

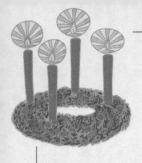

Family Puzzle

Do a jigsaw puzzle together. Set it up on a card table or another surface that you won't be needing regularly. Work on it from time to time throughout the holidays, a nonstressful and relaxing break in your holiday preparations.

The Sounds of Christmas

At a family gathering, make a tape recording from various times throughout the day. Listen to the recording at the end of the day and then save it to listen to at future Christmas celebrations.

Christmas Memories

Get the older members of your extended family to tell the younger ones (and everyone else) about Christmases from their childhood. The children learn about their heritage in this way, and it's a way of bringing the generations together.

Happy Birthday, Jesus!

Have a birthday cake for Jesus. Decorate the cake and put at least one candle on it. Sing "Happy Birthday" to Jesus before you blow out the candle. This is a good reminder of the reason we are celebrating Christmas.

We three kings of orient are,
Bearing gifts we traverse afar,
Field and fountain, moor and mountain,
Following yonder star.
O star of wonder, star of night,
Star with royal beauty bright;
Westward leading, still proceeding,
Guide us to thy perfect light!

JOHN HENRY HOPKINS, JR., 1862

New Foods

Serve a new dish each year. Make it a tradition every year to try a meal that you've never had before. Some will be more of a success than others, but your horizons will be expanded.

Christmas Scrapbook

After Christmas make a scrapbook. Include in it some of your Christmas cards, bulletins from the Christmas programs and services at church, photos, children's drawings, and anything else you would like to add. In years to come your family will be able to look back and remember what made this Christmas special.

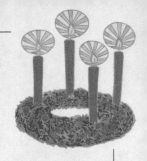

Be Realistic!

Don't try to do too much. Activities are great, but it's also important to take time to just *be* with people, instead of constantly *doing* things with them. If you spend too much time doing and going, the rush starts to make your activities less fun and more like work. To enjoy what you do, relax. Make it part of your family's Christmas tradition.

Fondue

Have a fondue supper for Christmas Eve. Dip bread, vegetables, and pieces of smoked sausage into cheese fondue for the first course. For dessert, have chocolate fondue with pieces of fruit.

*And the angel said unto them,
Fear not: for, behold,
I bring you good tidings of great joy,
which shall be to all people.
For unto you is born this day in the city of David a Saviour,
which is Christ the Lord.*

LUKE 2:10–11

Poinsettias

Buy lots of poinsettias and have your whole family help you arrange them around your home. Their brilliant color will make your home look cheery and Christmasy.

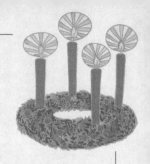

Animal Festivities

Let the pets get in on the Christmas festivities. Line the bird cage with wrapping paper or put a bow around the cat or dog's neck. Give your pet a special Christmas treat as well, like a spray of millet for the bird and fresh meat for the dog and cat. Children especially enjoy sharing Christmas joy with their feathered and furry friends.

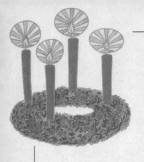

Advent Chain

Make a chain out of loops of red and green construction paper, 50 loops long. On the red loops write the names of friends and family to pray for, on the green loops write blessings that God has given you. Every day during Advent, take off one red loop

and one green one and use them in the prayers during your family devotions.

MATERIALS:
red and green construction paper   glue or staples
pencil or pen

Hail, the heaven-born Prince of Peace!
Hail the Sun of righteousness!
Light and life to all He brings,
Risen with healing in His wings;
Mild He lays his glory by;
Born that man no more may die;
Born to raise the sons of earth,
Born to give them second birth.

SAMUEL WESLEY, 1739

The Twelve Days of Christmas

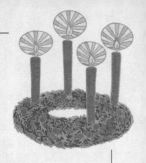

Keep track of the twelve days of Christmas, starting on December 26 and counting through January 6. This carries the celebrations past Christmas Day and helps ease out of the holidays, instead of having everything be abruptly over. It also celebrates Epiphany, January 6. This was the day that traditionally the Wise Men visited the baby Jesus. Make sure that your family has a special mini-celebration for each of the twelve days.

A Time for Music

Play a lot of Christmas music. It lets the Christmas atmosphere pervade your home.

Jesse Tree

This tree has ornaments that all relate to events that pointed to the coming of the Messiah and the people who were ancestors of Jesus. A ladder represents Jacob; little tablets, the law of Moses; and a scroll, Isaiah's prophecy. Use your knowledge of the Bible to come up with more ornament ideas, and ask your children for their help. This is a wonderful way to help your children understand the connection between Christmas and the Old Testament.

A Time to Worship

Attend at least one Christmas church service. Don't ever get too busy to participate in some of the services your church holds over the Christmas season. The Christmas Eve services are often especially beautiful, sometimes using candlelight. Let the peace of Christmas enfold you as you sing the songs and listen to the Scriptures. You may be tempted to say that your family is just too busy this year, but remember—Jesus is the reason for all our other Christmas activities. As families, we need to set aside some time to simply focus on Him.

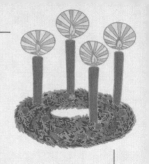

His name was called JESUS,
*which was so named of the angel
before he was conceived in the womb.*

LUKE 2:21

A Light for the Lonely

Place lighted candles in your windows. (You can get electric candles if you worry about fire.) This is an old German custom that welcomed those passing by and assured them that they would receive help if they were in need. Traditionally, on Christmas Eve, the candle was lit for Mary and Joseph on their way to Bethlehem, reminding families to open their hearts and homes to all those who were traveling or far from home.

Christmas Play

Act out the Christmas story with your family. Give everyone a part (or two, depending on the size of your family) and use a doll to represent the baby Jesus if you have no baby small enough. Use stuffed animals and toys for the sheep and other animals in the stable. Remember, you're never too old to play—and what better way to make the Christmas story come alive for your children?

Christmas Carols from Around the World

Learn traditional carols from around the world and try singing them together. You can find books of Christmas music in your local library. Remind your children that Jesus came not only for our country, but for the entire world.

Sledding

If there is enough snow during the Christmas holidays, take the family sledding—and make a memory your children will never forget. Choose a hill without many trees and away from roads. Make sure to have some hot chocolate ready when you come back home.

Still through the cloven skies they come,
With peaceful wings unfurled,
And still their heavenly music floats
O'er all the weary world;
Above its sad and lowly plains
They bend on hovering wing,
And ever o'er its Babel sounds
The blessed angels sing.

EDMUND HAMILTON SEARS, 1834

Focus on Christ

Instead of a tree, use a manger. Place a doll in a cradle or a wooden box. If you like, place the doll on a bed of evergreen branches instead of straw. Put your gifts around the manger as you would a tree. This makes sure that even your youngest children will understand that Jesus is truly at the center of Christmas.

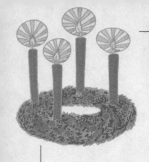

Fudge

Making fudge can be a whole-family activity. Be sure to make enough to share with neighbors and friends.

RECIPE:
²/3 cup evaporated milk

1 ²/3 cups sugar

¹/2 tsp salt

1 ¹/2 cups diced marshmallows

1 ¹/2 cups chocolate chips

1 tsp vanilla

Mix milk, sugar, and salt in a saucepan over low heat. Heat to boiling, then cook five minutes, stirring constantly. Remove from heat and add marshmallows, chocolate chips, and vanilla. Stir for 1 to 2 minutes, until marshmallows are melted. Pour into a greased square pan. Cool and cut into squares.

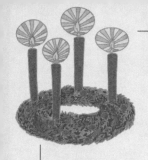

Twelfth Day Fun

Bake a Twelfth Day or Epiphany cake. Stir into the batter three hard beans (to symbolize the Three Wise Men), a toothpick (minstrel's baton), a foil star (for the astronomer), and enough almonds so that there will be something for everyone. After the cake has been eaten (make sure everyone is careful while eating) and the tokens found so that everyone has one, each person takes on the characteristics of the token they have, putting on costumes if you like. The Wise Men get places of honor and

the minstrel leads everyone in singing "We Three Kings." After that, the astronomer tells or reads the story of the Wise Men's visit to the Christ Child. The almonds represent servants, who get to clear up after supper.

MATERIALS:
cake mix (or bake a cake from scratch)   3 dried beans
1 toothpick   foil star
almonds

*A*nd when they had seen it,
they made known abroad the saying
which was told them concerning this child.
And all they that heard it wondered
at those things which were told them by the shepherds.

LUKE 2:17–18

A Christmas Play

Go see a production of *Amahl and the Night Visitors*. This beautiful Christmas play is suitable even for young children.

"Snow"

Make artificial snow for decorations. Use powdered detergent and only a tiny bit of water, beating it until it's stiff and fluffy. Trim your windows or tree with the "snow," or make it into balls

before it hardens, inserting an ornament hook as soon as you form the ball. The snow washes off windows easily.

MATERIALS:
powdered detergent water

Christmas Surprises

Do something special for someone who is not expecting it. This could mean shoveling their driveway and steps, making them a loaf of banana bread, or leaving a Christmas present in their mailbox. Make sure your children are a part of the fun.

A-Caroling We Go

Go caroling with a group of other families from your church. Decide beforehand where you plan to go. Finish at someone's house with hot chocolate and cookies.

Candles

Make candles—for gifts or for your family's Christmas use. Use juice cans or milk cartons for molds and cord for wicks. Melt paraffin, then add stearic acid or beeswax before pouring the wax into the molds. Color can be added with your children's old crayons. Encourage your children to think of decorations to press into the outsides of the candles—buttons, pebbles, shells, dried flowers, etc.

MATERIALS:
paraffin
old crayons
assorted hard objects (pretty stones, shells, etc.)

stearic acid or beeswax
juice cans or milk cartons

A Delicious Tradition

Decorate Christmas cookies together. Get as many colors of frosting and as many different kinds of decorator sugars and sprinkles as you can. Everyone try to make their cookies creative and colorful.

Joy to the earth! The Savior reigns;
Let men their songs employ;
While fields and floods, rocks, hills and plains
Repeat the sounding joy.

ISAAC WATTS, 1719

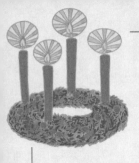

Snowmen

If you live where you have enough snow, go outside with your children and make a snowman together. Make sure your snowman gets his carrot nose; find stones to make his eyes and mouth.

Crazy Gift Exchange

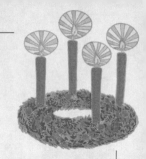

Wrap enough small gifts so there's enough for everyone in your family to get one. Sit in a circle and give everyone a gift. Start the Christmas music. Everyone passes the gifts to their right until the music stops. Then they start tearing the wrapping paper off until the music starts again (like musical chairs). When a person unwraps a gift completely, they get to keep it. Use lots of wrapping paper and tape.

Candlelight Blessing

Put a candle for each member of the family on the table. Light the candles one at a time, thanking God for that person and asking His blessing on them.

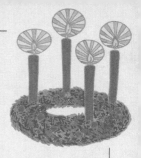

The Blessing of Giving

Don't let your children get too caught up in all the things they want to get for Christmas. Teach them that it is more blessed to give than to receive. Over Christmas vacation, encourage them to clean out their rooms and share unneeded toys and clothing with those who are less fortunate.

And of his fulness have all we received,
and grace for grace.

JOHN 1:16

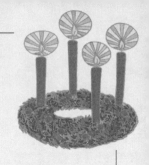

Fund-raisers

Support local fund-raising Christmas sales. You will be helping out a good cause and you can probably pick up a few gifts at the same time. These are great places for children to do their Christmas shopping, too.

Break a Tradition

Sometimes it's nice not to have a big dinner on Christmas Day. Have your special meal on another day and spend Christmas Day quietly, without rushing around.

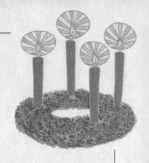

A Little at a Time

Decorate the house a little at a time. Starting at the beginning of Advent, decorate one part of your home. Keep adding decorations as it gets closer to Christmas. The anticipation of seeing the house become more and more decorated can be better than doing it all at once. Encourage your whole family to participate.

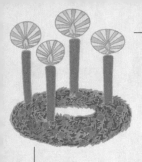

Let There Be Light!

String colored lights around all the windows. Put lots of lights on the tree. Decorate a couple of outside trees with lights as well. Jesus is the light of the world—have a celebration of light this year.

For Christ is born of Mary;
And gathered all above,
While mortals sleep, the angels keep
Their watch of wondering love.
O morning stars, together
Proclaim the holy birth!
And praises sing to God the King,
And peace to men on earth.

PHILLIPS BROOKS, 1868

Luminaries

Make luminaries to set on your porch or at the end of your sidewalk. Set a votive candle in the bottom of a small white bakery bag and anchor it with sand or kitty litter. If you like, punch

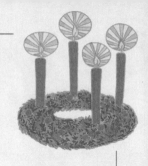

holes in the sides of the bag to create a design for the light to shine through. This idea works best if you have no snow.

MATERIALS:
candles   sand or kitty litter
small white paper bags

Surprises in the Mail

Mail your children several little gifts. Let them open the gifts right away. Everyone loves getting mail, especially unexpected gifts.

Stockings

Make stockings for all the members of the family. Get the children to help by choosing the fabric and trim they would like for their stocking. If they are old enough, they can help put the stockings together as well.

herefore the Lord himself
shall give you a sign;
Behold, a virgin shall conceive, and bear a son,
and shall call his name Immanuel.
Butter and honey shall he eat,
that he may know to refuse the evil,
and choose the good.

ISAIAH 7:14–15

Star Light, Star Bright

Have a star theme for supper one night. Try to make and arrange as many of the foods as you can into a star shape. Use star-shaped ice cubes colored with red and green food coloring. Have star cookies for dessert. Sprinkle silver stars across the tablecloth.

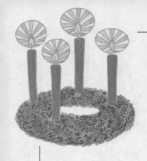

Christmas Greetings

Help children make their own Christmas cards for relatives and friends. Let them personalize the cards with artwork, photos, or notes.

MATERIALS:

red or green construction paper
scissors
crayons or markers

old Christmas cards
glue
pens or pencils

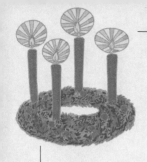

"Crackers"

This is a tradition that comes from England. Use the cardboard tubes from toilet paper and cover them with fabric or several layers of tissue paper. Fill the crackers with candy or a small gift and tie off the ends with ribbons. Place one cracker at each plate at your Christmas meal.

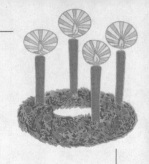

MATERIALS:
toilet paper tubes
ribbons
small gifts

Christmas fabric or
tissue paper

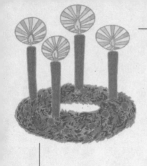

Silent night! Holy night!
Shepherds quake at the sight;
Glories stream from heaven afar,
Heavenly hosts sing, "Alleluia,
Christ, the Savior, is born,
Christ, the Savior, is born."

JOSEPH MOHR, 1818

Sweet Memories

Make Christmas cupcakes. Decorate them with miniature candy canes or with snowmen cut out of marshmallows. Use cinnamon candy to make holly berries or poinsettia leaves.

Unique Decorations

Buy clear glass Christmas balls and have family members decorate them with acrylic paint. Use makeup brushes or cotton swabs to apply the paint. Make sure everyone signs their artwork.

MATERIALS:
clear glass Christmas balls
makeup brushes or cotton swabs

gold acrylic paint

Christmas
Away from Home

Meet at a camp for your extended family gathering. This way there's room for everyone and no one has to cook, since meals are provided by the staff. Bring along whatever treats you want to make the time special.

*For God so loved the world,
that he gave his only begotten Son,
that whosoever believeth in him should not perish,
but have everlasting life.*

JOHN 3:16

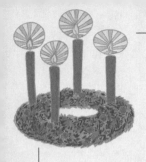

Natural Decorations

Make decorations out of items from nature such as pinecones, acorns, and berries. Work together to collect items and decide how they are to be used. Get everyone to help with the creation of the decorations.

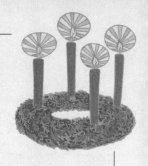

MATERIALS:
pinecones
acorns
dried teasels

gold or silver spray paint
glue
Christmas ribbon

Share Your Bounty

For a week during Advent, eat only bread and soup. Teach the children about people who don't have as much food as we do. At the end of the week, send the money you have saved from meals to a relief organization that you have chosen.

T̲hen let us all with one accord
Sing praises to our heavenly Lord,
That hath made heaven and earth of naught,
And with His blood mankind hath bought.

ANONYMOUS, 17TH CENTURY

Work Together

Get everyone to help with the making of Christmas dinner. The work shouldn't be left to only one person—and a lot of conversation and fellowship can occur when everyone is working together.

Christmas Witness

Put a nativity scene and cross on your front lawn. Set up a spotlight so that it can be seen well at night.

Christmas Baking

Do a lot of Christmas baking, with everyone helping out. Wrap your baked goods in boxes or with colored cellophane. Deliver them in person to friends and neighbors. This way people won't just get the benefit of your baking, they'll get to see your family and visit with you as well.

Alternative Christmas Trees

Instead of using a real cut tree or an artificial tree bought in a department store, try other possibilities, such as the branch of a deciduous tree, a small potted tree, or vines and moss wrapped over a framework.

*I*n this was manifested the love of God toward us, because that God sent his only begotten Son into the world, that we might live through him.

1 JOHN 4:9

Christmas Treasure Hunt

On Christmas Eve, set up a treasure hunt for your children, leading to a present. Give easy clues for the younger ones and make the clues a little more difficult for older children. Leave a candy cane or cookie beside some of the clues.

Rise and Shine

Wake your children up on school mornings in December by playing Christmas music. They still might not want to go to school, but they will probably wake up happier.

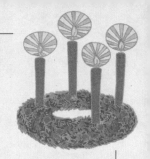

A Special Christmas

Even if you don't have very much money this Christmas, try to make the season special. You don't have to spend a lot of money on decorations or gifts, just use what you have and make gifts of time when you can't manage buying for everyone. Most of all, make a point this Christmas to do things together as a family. The joy of Christmas has nothing to do with material wealth and everything to do with the Christ-like spirit that shines as we share our love with each other.

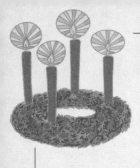

Christmas All Year Long

Keep some of the Christmas spirit in your heart throughout the year. As a family, perform acts of kindness to each other and to those outside your family, not just at Christmas but all year long. Remind your children that the true spirit of Christmas lasts for eternity.

*A*way in a manger, no crib for a bed,
The little Lord Jesus laid down His sweet head.
The stars in the bright sky looked down where He lay,
The little Lord Jesus asleep on the hay.

ANONYMOUS

Beloved, if God so loved us,
we ought also to love one another.

1 JOHN 4:11

Christmas is a time for families, a time for being with children, a time for fun and merriment. Thank God for the special gift of our families! As busy grown-ups, we need to remember that all our activities—at Christmas time and all year round—should center on sharing the love of Christ with those around us. Even the simplest activities can become a heritage of love, stored up in our children's memories for them to share one day with their own families.

G od bless the master of this house,
The mistress bless also,
And all the little children
That round the table go;

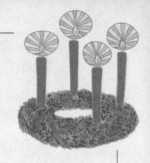

*A*nd all your kin and kinsmen,
That dwell both far and near;
I wish you a Merry Christmas,
And a happy New Year.

ANONYMOUS

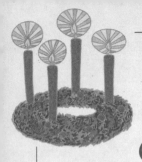

What I'd like to have for Christmas
I can tell you in a minute.
The family all around me,
And the home with laughter in it.

EDGAR A. GUEST